The Top 1,000 Words
for Understanding
Media Arabic

The Top 1,000 Words for Understanding Media Arabic

Elisabeth Kendall

Georgetown University Press
Washington, D.C.

Georgetown University Press
Washington, D.C.

10 9 8 7 6 5 4   2006

This volume is printed on acid-free offset book paper.

First published in the United Kingdom by
Edinburgh University Press.

Library of Congress Cataloging-in-Publication Data

Kendall, Elisabeth.
 The top 1,000 words for understanding media Arabic / Elisabeth Kendall.
    p. cm.
 English and Arabic.
 ISBN 1-58901-068-X (alk. paper)
1. Arabic language—Terms and phrases. 2. Arabic language—Glossaries,
vocabularies, etc. 3. Mass media—Terminology. I. Title: Top one
thousand words for understanding media Arabic. II. Title.
 PJ6680.K42 2005
 492.7′2—dc22

                              2005040059

Typeset in Times New Roman and Geeza Pro
and printed and bound in Germany.

CONTENTS

INTRODUCTION

The ability to access Media Arabic – the language of printed or broadcast news items – has become increasingly important in the light of recent developments in the Middle East. Consequently, the need for a 'quick-fix' vocabulary of Media Arabic is greater than ever. Arabic dictionaries are not equipped to deal with Media Arabic which involves many new coinages to express contemporary concepts (for example, multi-culturalism, anti-aircraft missile, globalisation). While English-speaking students can deduce some terms from Arabic to English by thinking laterally (for example, ministerial straightening equals cabinet reshuffle, the falsification of elections equals election-rigging), this is a much more hit-and-miss process when attempted from English to Arabic. Until now, getting to know the Arabic for common contemporary media terminology has necessitated a long period of familiarisation with the Arabic media. This book is designed to help undergraduates, postgraduates, governmental, military, diplomatic and business personnel bypass this lengthy process.

This book aims to supply the core vocabulary of Media Arabic in a logical format to provide easy reference and easy-to-learn lists testing both Arabic to English and English to Arabic. Familiarisation with this book will furnish the reader with an invaluable knowledge of the key vocabulary components essential to comprehend, translate, write and speak contemporary Media Arabic. Whilst independently useful, this book is best used in conjunction with Julia Ashtiany's excellent *Media Arabic* (EUP, 1993), a coursebook which sets the vocabulary in context and teaches students to manipulate typical Media Arabic structures and formats.

This book comprises eight sections, organised by topic: General; Politics; Elections; Military; Economics; Trade and Industry; Law and Order; and Disaster and Aid. The initial General section comprises vocabulary pertaining to reports, statements, sources and common media idioms of a general nature. Prepositions and idiomatic time expressions are listed only where particular variations arise in Media Arabic. For example, 'day', 'week' and so on are excluded whereas 'in the long term', 'in the near future' are included. Generally, basic vocabulary such as would be acquired during elementary grammatical training is excluded. The General and Politics sections are naturally the longest, since much of this vocabulary is also used in media discussions concerning the Military, Economics, Trade and Industry and so on. Vocabulary is not repeated except where this forms part of an expression to produce a new meaning. Expressions have been excluded where the reader has the information to assemble these logically. For example, 'intelligence' and 'military' are both supplied as general media vocabulary items in the General section, therefore 'military intelligence' does not feature as a separate entry in the Military section.

Each section has its own internal logic. For example, the Politics section begins with common political acronyms and organisations followed by political systems, descriptors of political stance, political bodies and organisations, political offices and roles, geographical entities, and so on. Direct subtitles for groupings within each section have been avoided since not all vocabulary items can be neatly categorised beyond the broad section title. Within each logical grouping, alphabetical order has purposely been avoided since this has a negative impact on the learning of vocabulary lists. Lastly, this book does not claim to be exhaustive and the choice of vocabulary is necessarily to some extent subjective. However, every effort has been made to select the most useful and/or common vocabulary items.

Notes on the formal presentation

The Arabic is vocalised to ensure correct pronunciation and entrench in the mind the vocalisation patterns of certain structures. However, short vowels are not supplied where:
- a fatha precedes a long alif or a ta' marbuta
- a kasra precedes a long ya
- a damma precedes a long waw

The pronunciation of sun and moon letters is assumed knowledge and has not been marked.

End vowels have not been supplied where they are not generally pronounced or where they vary for case.

In general, Arabic nouns are supplied in both the singular and plural; the plural is printed after the comma.

A circular ha is shown to indicate the location of the direct object in cases where verbs take prepositions after the direct object.

Where '+ idafah' is written in the text, this indicates that the Arabic must be followed by the genitive construction.

First form verbs

These have been supplied in the form of the basic stem (past tense masculine singular) followed by the present tense (masculine singular with the middle vowel marked) and the masdar (verbal noun). The middle vowel of the past tense has only been supplied where this is not a fatha. Where two short vowels are marked with the same letter, this indicates that both are possible.

Derived forms of the verb

These have been supplied only in the form of the basic stem (past tense masculine singular), since present tense vocalisation and masdars are predictable for derived forms of the verb. The present tense and masdars have been supplied only where the spelling of the verb changes significantly (for example, the present tense of second form first radical hamza verbs), where a separate vocabulary item is intended, or where the word is commonly misvocalised.

Abbreviations

s.t.	something
s.o.	someone
pl.	plural
lit.	literally

1. GENERAL

وَسائِل الإعْلام	the media
الصِحافة	the press
وكالة الأنْباء	press agency
صِحافيّ \ صُحُفيّ، –ون	journalist
صَحيفة، صُحُف \ صَحائِف	newspaper
جَريدة، جَرائِد	"
مُقابَلة، –ات	interview
مُؤْتَمَر صُحُفيّ \ صَحَفيّ	press conference
مَصْدَر، مَصادِر	source
مَصادِر مُطَّلِعة	informed sources
مَصادِر مُقَرَّبة مِن	sources close to
مَصادِر مَوْثوق بِها	reliable/trusted sources
مَصادِر عالية المُسْتَوَى	high-level sources
عَدَم كَشْف الهُويّة	anonymity
قال يَقول قَوْل	to say
قيل يُقال	it was/is said
أضاف يُضيف إضافة	to add

واصَل	to continue
ما زال، لَمْ يَزَلْ، لا يَزال	to continue, carry on (lit. not to cease)
اِسْتَطْرَد	to go on to say
ذكر يذكُر ذكْر	to mention, recall
أكَّد يُؤَكِّد تَأْكيد	to confirm
نفَى ينفي نَفْي	to refute, deny, repudiate
أنْكَر	to deny
اِسْتَبْعَد	to rule out; to regard as unlikely
صَرَّح بِ	to state
أعْرَب \ عَبَّر عَن	to express
أعْلَن	to declare, announce
زعم يزعُم زَعْم	to claim
نقل ينقُل نَقْل	to communicate, convey
أوْرَد	to state, quote, convey
طرح يطرَح طَرْح آراءَهُ	to present one's opinions
أفاد يُفيد إفادة ه بِ	to notify, inform s.o. of s.t.
أبْلَغ ه بِ \ عَن	to tell, inform s.o. about s.t.
أطْلَع ه عَلَى	to tell s.o. s.t.

أَدْلَى إِلَى بِ	to let s.o. know s.t., inform s.o. of s.t.
رأى يَرَى رَأْي \ رُؤْية	to deem, consider
اعْتَبَر	"
عدَّ يعُدّ عَدّ	"
اعْتَقَد	to believe
عَلَّق عَلَى	to comment on
أَلْقَى خِطاباً	to give a speech
أَصْدَر	to publish, express, issue
أذاع يُذيع إذاعة	to broadcast
وصف يَصِف وَصْف ه بِ	to describe s.t./s.o. as
أَوْضَح	to elucidate, clarify
شرح يشرَح شَرْح	"
أَلْقَى الضَّوْء عَلَى	to throw light on
صدر يصدُر صُدور	to be published
نشر ينشُر نَشْر	to propagate, spread, publicise, publish
انْتَشَر	to be widespread
رَدّ يرُدّ رَدّ عَلَى	to respond to
أَجاب يُجيب إجابة عَلَى	to answer, respond to s.t.

أَجاب يُجيب إِجابة ه \ إِلَى	to answer, respond to s.o.
اسْتَجْوَب	to interrogate, examine
اسْتَفْهَم ه عن	to inquire, ask s.o. about
سأَل يسأَل سُؤال	to ask
أَشار يُشير إِشارة إِلَى	to indicate, point to
لَمَّح \ أَلْمَح إِلَى	to hint at, allude to
اقْتَرَح	to suggest, propose
افْتَرَض	to assume, presume
افْتَرَض عَلَى ه	to impose upon s.o. s.t.
أَصَرَّ عَلَى	to insist on
اسْتَعْرَض	to survey, review
حَدَّد	to define
رَكَّز عَلَى	to concentrate, focus on
شَدَّد عَلَى	to emphasise, stress
سمَح يسمَح سَماح لِ بِ	to allow, permit s.o. s.t.
وَصَّى يُوَصِّي تَوْصية ه بِ	to advise
أَوْصَى ه بِ	"
نصَح ينصَح نَصْح ه بِ	"
شاوَر	to consult

اِشْتَرَط	to stipulate
طالَب ه \ ب	to demand, request
جَدير بِالذِكْر أَن	worth mentioning is the fact that
حَذَّر ه مِن	to warn s.o. about
أَنْذَر ه بِ	"
حَذِر يحذَر حِذْر \ حَذَر	to be cautious, wary of
اِحْتَذَر	"
شَكّ يشُكّ شَكّ في \ بِ	to doubt, suspect
تَـجنَّب	to avoid
أَشاد بِ	to praise
اِنْتَقَد	to criticise
نَدَّد بِ	"
قَوَّم	to evaluate
أَثار الشُكوك حَوْلَ	to raise doubts about
عِبْء الإِثْبات يَقَع عَلَى	the burden of proof falls on
أَقَرّ بِ	to admit, confess
اِعْتَرَف بِ	"
كَشف يكشِف كَشْف ه\عَن	to expose, reveal

دلّ يدُلّ دَلالة عَلَى	to show, prove
عرض يعرِض عَرْض	to show, demonstrate
أَظْهَر	"
أَساء يُسيىء إساءة	to harm the image of
إلَى صورة	(+ idafah)
اكْتَشف	to discover
عكس يعكس عَكْس	to reflect
كفل يكفُل كَفْل \ كُفول \	to guarantee
كَفالة	
أَجْرَى اتِّصالاً هاتِفيّاً بـ	to make a phone call to
شارَك في	to participate in
ساهَم في	to contribute to
لَعَب يلعَب لَعْب دَوْراً في	to play a role in
سبَّب	to cause
أَنْتَج	to cause, provoke, give rise to
أثار يُثير إثارة	to provoke, incite, arouse
أثَّر يؤَثِّر تَأْثير	to influence
تَأَثَّر	to be influenced
أدَّى يُؤَدِّي تَأْدية إلَى	to lead to

أَسْفَر عَن	to result in
مَهَّد الطَريق	to pave the way
رجع يرجِع رُجوع إلَى	to go back to, stem from
نَتيجة	as a result of (+ idafah)
بِسَبَب	"
طبع يطبَع طَبْع	to impress
اِنْطَبَع	to be impressed
بحث يبحَث بَحْث ه \ عَن	to explore, investigate; to discuss
ناقَش	to discuss
باحَث	"
تَبادَل	to exchange (e.g. views)
تَعاوَن	to cooperate
تَناوَل	to treat, deal with s.t.
عامَل	to treat, deal with s.o.
شمَِل يشمَل شمَل \ شُمول	to incorporate, take in, include
اِنْضَمّ	to comprise, include
اِنْضَمّ إلى	to join
وُجْهة النَظَر، –ات النَظَر	point of view

سِياق	context
ساحة، ‒ات	area, field
مَجال، ‒ات	"
مَيدان، مَيادين	"
صَعيد، صُعُد	level, plane
مُسْتَوَى، مُسْتَوَيات	"
طَريقة، طَرائِق \ طُرُق	method, way
سَبيل، سُبُل	"
وَسيلة، وَسائِل	means
وَفْقاً لِ	according to
نَقْلاً عَن	"
طِبْقاً لِ	"
عَلَى حَسَب	" (+ idafah)
حَسْبَما	according to (+ verb)
عَلَى غِرار	in the manner of, on the pattern of (+ idafah)
ما إذا	whether
عَلَناً	publicly
في إطار	in the framework of (+ idafah)
عَلَى أَساس	on the basis of (+ idafah)

بَدَلاً مِن	instead of
بِخِلاف	other than, besides (+ idafah)
مُقابِلَ	in exchange for; in relation to, in comparison with
بِما في ذلِك	including
عَلَى صَعيدٍ آخَر	on the other hand
مِن جِهةٍ أُخْرَى	"
مِن ناحيةٍ أُخْرَى	"
مِن جانِبٍ آخَر	"
فيما يَتَعَلَّق بِ	with regard to
مِن ناحية	from the point of view of, with regard to (+ idafah)
بِالنِسْبة إلَى	with regard to
نَظَراً إلَى لِ	in view of, with regard to
في هذا الصَدَد	in this respect
وَجْه، وُجوه \ أوْجُه	aspect, approach, standpoint
إزاءَ	in the face of, towards
تُجاه	towards
لا يَجِب أن ... طالما أن	it doesn't have to ... as long as

إلَى حَدٍّ ما	to some extent
إلَى دَرَجة أَنَّ	to the extent that
عَلَى حَدٍّ سَواء	equally
مِن أَجْل	for the sake of (+ idafah)
بِفَضْل	thanks to (+ idafah)
مُجَرَّد	mere, pure (+ idafah)
مما يَعْني أن	meaning that
بِمَعْنَى أن	"
بِفَحْوَى أن	"
عَلَى الساحة الدَوليّة	on the international stage
في مُخْتَلِف أَنْحاء العالَم	in various parts of the world
في كُلِّ أَنْحاء العالَم	all over the world
إمْكانيّة، –ات	possibility
احْتِمال، –ات	eventuality, probability
مِن المُحْتَمَل أن	it is likely/probable that
مِن المُمْكِن أن	it is possible that
مِن الواضِح أن	it is clear that
مِن المُنْتَظَر أن	it is anticipated that
مِن المُتَوَقَّع أن	it is expected that

مِن الضَّروريّ أَن	it is necessary to
مِن اللازِم أَن	"
مِن الواجِب أَن	"
مِن المُسْتَحيل أَن	it is inconceivable that
لا يُسْتَبْعَد أَن	it is not inconceivable that
لا بُدَّ مِن أَن	it is inevitable/essential that
قَرار، ‑ات	decision
قَرار الأُمَـم المُتَّحِدة	UN resolution
جَدْوَل الأعْمال	agenda
مَشْروع، ‑ات \ مَشاريع	plan, project
خُطّة، خُطَط	plan
إعْلان، ‑ات	declaration, announcement
بَيان، ‑ات	statement, declaration, communique, manifesto
تَصْريح، ‑ات	statement
إشارة، ‑ات	indication, sign
مَعْلومات	information (Arabic pl.)
اِسْتِخْبارات	intelligence (Arabic pl.)
تَحْقيق، ‑ات	investigation
تَقْرير، تَقارير	report, account

تَحْليل، –ات	analysis
إيضاح، –ات	explanation, clarification
شَرْح	elucidation, explanation
تَعْليل، –ات	argumentation, justification
تَبْرير، –ات	justification, vindication
وَصْف، أَوْصاف	description
أَمْر، أُمور	matter; order
قَضية، قَضايا	issue, affair, matter, question
مَسْأَلة، مَسائِل	"
واقِعة، وَقائِع	occurrence, incident
حَدَث، أَحْداث	event, occurrence
سِلْسِلة أَحْداث	chain of events
مُناسَبَة، –ات	occasion, opportunity
فُرْصة، فُرَص	opportunity
شَأْن، شُؤون	matter, affair
وَضْع، أَوْضاع	position
مَوْقِف، مَواقِف	position, stance
حال، أَحْوال	circumstance, state, condition
ظُروف	circumstances

مَأْزِق، مَازِق	impasse, predicament
مَوْعِد، مَواعِد	date; appointment
ميعاد، مَواعيد	"
تاريخ، تَواريخ	date; history
مَقْصِد، مَقاصِد	intention, aim
نيّة، نَوايا	"
هَدَف، أَهْداف	aim, objective
غَرَض، أَغْراض	target, aim, goal
طُمُوح	ambition
رامٍ إلَى	aiming at
نَتيجة، نَتائِج	result
عُقْب، أَعْقاب	upshot, outcome
عاقِبة، عَواقِب	consequence, outcome
عَقَبة، –ات \ عِقاب	impediment, obstacle
تَأْثير، –ات	influence
أَثَر	"
نُفُوذ	"
سَبَب، أَسْباب	cause, reason
مَبْعَث، مَباعِث	cause, factor

مُبَرِّر، –ات	justification, excuse
دافِع، دَوافِع	motive
دَوافِع	dynamics (Arabic pl.)
عامِل، عَوامِل	factor
عُنْصُر، عَناصِر	element
حَقيقة، حَقائِق	fact; reality, truth

Adjectives

سياسيّ	political
ثَقافيّ	cultural
دينيّ	religious
اِجْتِماعيّ	social
زِراعيّ	agricultural
فِكْريّ	intellectual
اِقْتِصاديّ	economic
ماليّ	financial
عَسْكَريّ	military
رَسْميّ	official
غَيْر رَسْميّ	unofficial

مَدَنيّ	civil
اسْتِشاريّ	advisory
شَعْبيّ	popular
قَوْميّ	national, people's (i.e. of the people)
أُمَـميّ	UN (adj.)
تِجاريّ	commercial
صِناعيّ	industrial; artificial
إقْليميّ	regional
مَحَلّيّ	local
مِهْنيّ	professional
إداريّ	administrative
عاطِفيّ	emotional
أساسيّ	fundamental, basic
جِذْريّ	"
هَيْكَليّ	structural
سَلْبيّ	negative
إيجابيّ	positive
تفاؤُليّ	optimistic
تشاؤُمىّ	pessimistic

عَمَليّ	practical
نَظَريّ	theoretical
شَفَويّ	oral
خَطّيّ	written
فِعْليّ	factual, actual; efficient; practical
حَقيقيّ	real
واقِعيّ	realistic, real
عارٍ \عارية تماماً مِن الصِحّة	completely untrue
عاديّ	ordinary
مَعْني \ مُرْتَبَك	implicated, concerned, involved
جُزْئيّ	partial
واسِع النِطاق	far-reaching
شامِل	comprehensive
كامِل	entire, complete
وَطيد	firm, solid
مَضْمون	guaranteed
غَيْر مَسْبوق	unprecedented

مَعْروف حَتَّى الآن بِ	hitherto known as
شَهير \ مَشْهور	famous, well-known
بارِز	prominent
مُعَيَّن	specific
مُمَيَّز	distinct
خاصّ	private, special
عامّ	general, public
مُتَفاوِت	various
مُخْتَلِف	different
عادِل	just
مُتَوازِن	balanced
مَسْؤول	responsible
غَيْر مَسْؤول	irresponsible
مُسيء إلَى	harmful to
مَهْزول، مَهازيل	degenerate, weak
مُفْتَعَل	spurious, forged
مُعَقَّد	complicated, complex
حَذِر	cautious
مَشْروع	legitimate

مَلْموس	tangible
مُهِمّ \ هامّ	important
مِحْوَرِيّ	pivotal
حاسِم	decisive, crucial, definitive
حَرِج	critical, crucial
خَطير	significant, grave
آلِيّ	instrumental
جادّ	serious
بالِغ الأهَمِّيّة	of the utmost importance
عَلَى جانِبٍ كَبيرٍ مِن الأهَمِّيّة	"
في المَقامِ الأوَّل	"
ذو \ ذات الاهْتِمامِ المُشْتَرَك	of mutual significance
مُثير لِلْجَدَل	controversial
رَئيسِيّ	main, principal
شائِع	widespread
سائِد	prevailing
رائِج	current, widespread, universal
ساحِق	overwhelming
مُتَوافِق مَع	compatible with

مُلائِم	suitable, appropriate
مُشابِه	similar

Time expressions

عَلَى المَدَى البَعيد	in the long term
عَلَى المَدَى القَريب	in the short term
أسْرَع ما يُمْكِن	as quickly as possible
في أسْرَع وَقْت مُمْكِن	as soon as possible
سابِق	former
ماضٍ \ الماضي	past
حالِيّ	present, current
جارٍ \ الجاري	"
راهِن	"
مُقبِل	future, forthcoming
قادِم	"
قائِم	existing, existent
أخير	recent; final
نِهائِيّ	final
وَشيك	imminent

دائِم	permanent
مُؤَقَّت	temporary, interim
خاطِف	fleeting
عَلَى التَّوالي	continuously
أَخيراً	recently; finally
قَريباً	soon
عادةً	usually
نادِراً	rarely
كَثيراً	often
أَحْياناً	sometimes
في نَفْسِ الوَقْت	at the same time, simultaneously
في المسْتَقْبَلِ القَريب	in the near future
خِلالَ	during
أَثْناءَ	"
قَبْلَ	before
قُبَيْلَ	shortly before
بَعْدَ \ عَقِبَ	after
بُعَيْدَ	shortly after

في أَعْقاب   in the wake of (+ idafah)

فيما بَعْد   subsequently

فَوْرَ   as soon as

في هذه الأَثْناء   meanwhile

بِتَوْقيت جرينتش   GMT (Greenwich Mean Time)

2. POLITICS

مَجْلِس التَعاوُنِ الخَليجيّ	GCC (Gulf Cooperation Council)
الأُمَم المُتَّحِدة	UN (United Nations)
الجَمْعيّة العامّة	The (UN) General Assembly
يونَسْكو	UNESCO (United Nations Educational, Scientific and Cultural Organisation)
مُنَظَّمة الاتِّحاد الأُورُبّيّ	EU (European Union)
حلِف شَمَالِ الأَطْلَسيّ	NATO (North Atlantic Treaty Organisation)
الأَطْلَسيّ	"
الوِكالة الدَوليّة للطاقة الذَريّة	IAEA (International Atomic Energy Authority)
مُنَظَّمة التَحْرير الفِلَسْطينيّة	PLO (Palestinian Liberation Organisation)
جامِعة الدُوَل العَرَبيّة	the Arab League
الرابِطة الإسْلاميّة	the Muslim League
مُنَظَّمة المُؤْتَمَر الإسْلاميّ	OIC (the Organisation of the Islamic Conference)
الإخْوان المُسْلِمون	the Muslim Brotherhood

المُؤْتمَر اليَهوديّ العالَميّ	WJC (the World Jewish Congress)
الكنيست	the Knesset
جَبْهة الإِنْقاذ الإِسْلاميّ	the Islamic Salvation Front
مُنَظَّمة الوَحْدة الإفْريقيّة	OAU (the Organisation of African Unity)
مَجْلِس الأمْن	the Security Council
الدُوَل الخَمْس ذات العُضْويّة الدَائِمة في مَجْلِسِ الأمْن	the Five Permanent Member States of the Security Council
المُجْتَمَع الدَوليّ	the international community
مِحْوَر الشَرّ	Axis of Evil
جَماعة السَلامِ الأخْضَر	Greenpeace
هَيْئة الصَليبِ الأحْمَر	the Red Cross
هَيْئة الهِلالِ الأحْمَر	the Red Crescent
مُنَظَّمة العَفْوِ الدَوليّة	Amnesty International
حزْب العُمّال	the Labour Party
حزْب المُحافظين	the Conservative Party
اللّيبِراليّون	the Liberals
الحزْب الدّيموقراطيّ	the Democrats

الحِزْب الجُمْهوريّ	the Republicans
اليَمين	the Right
اليَسار	the Left
الأَدَوات السياسيّة	the political apparatus
تَحَفُّظ	conservatism
ليبراليّة	liberalism
تَعَدُّديّة	pluralism
تَعَدُّديّة ثَقافيّة	multi-culturalism
مُعاداة الساميّة	anti-semitism
رَأْسْماليّة	capitalism
اشْتِراكيّة	socialism
شُيوعيّة	communism
شُموليّة	totalitarianism
إقْطاعيّة	feudalism
نازيّة جَديدة	neo-Nazism
صَهْيونيّة	Zionism
عُنْصُريّة	racism
تَطَرُّف	extremism
إرْهاب	terrorism

فَئَوِيّة	factionalism
انْفِصاليّة	separatism
مَذْهَبِيّة \ طائِفيّة	sectarianism
أُصوليّة	fundamentalism
حُكْم ذاتيّ	self-rule, autonomy
تَقْرير مَصيرِه \ ها	self-determination
نِظام الحِزْبِ الواحِد	one-party system
نِظام الأَحْزابِ المُتَعَدِّدة	multi-party system
حُكْم لا مَرْكَزيّ	decentralised rule
مَلَكيّة دُسْتوريّة	constitutional monarchy
اشْتِراكيّ	socialist
شُموليّ	totalitarian
شُيوعيّ	communist
رَأْسْماليّ	capitalist
أَساسيّ \ أُصوليّ	fundamentalist
صَهْيونيّ	Zionist
عَلْمانيّ	secularist
انْفِصاليّ	separatist
مَذْهَبيّ \ طائِفيّ	sectarian

فِئَوِيّ	factional
دُسْتُورِيّ	constitutional
غَيْر دُسْتُورِيّ	unconstitutional
ديموقراطيّ	democratic
نَخْبَوِيّ	electoral
قَبَلِيّ	tribal
عِرْقِيّ	racial
مُتَطَرِّف	extremist
مُتَشَدِّد	radical, bigot
مُتَصَلِّب	hard-line
ثَوْرِيّ	revolutionary
يَمِينِيّ	right-wing
يَسارِيّ	left-wing, leftist
مُحايِد	neutral
اتِّحاد، –ات	union
رابِطة، رَوابِط	confederation, league
تَحالُف	(state of) alliance
مَجْلِس، مَجالِس	council
جَمْعِيّة، –ات	society, club, assembly

شَبَكة، –ات	network
تَكَتُّل	bloc
جَبْهة، جَبَهات	front
لَجْنة، –ات \ لِجان	committee, commission, board, council
هَيْئة، –ات	board, council, commission
مُعارَضة	opposition
مُقاوَمة	resistance
حِزْب، أَحْزاب	party
حِزْب حاكِم	ruling party
جِناح، أَجْنِحة	wing
حُكومة، –ات	government
حُكومة مُؤَقَّتة	caretaker/interim government
حُكومة انْتِقاليّة	transition government, provisional government
صُفوف القِيادة	leadership ranks
بَرْلَمان	parliament
مَقَرّ المَكْتَبِ السياسيّ	the political headquarters
قَصْر، قُصور	palace
بَلاط	court (royal)

مُنَظَّمة \ تَنْظيم، –ات	organisation
مُؤَسَّسة، –ات	establishment, foundation
سُلْطة	authority
السُّلُطات	the authorities
سُلْطة مُؤَقَّتة	interim authority
حُكْم	rule
نِظام، أَنْظِمة	regime
رِئَاسة	leadership
وَفْد، وُفود	delegation
طاقِم، طَواقِم	team, crew
فِرقة الوِساطة، فِرَق الوِساطة	team of mediators
مَبْعوث، –ون	delegate, envoy
مَنْدوب، –ون	delegate, agent, representative
مُمَثِّل، –ون	representative
مَسْؤول، –ون	official
كِبار المسْؤولين	high-ranking officials
مُفَتِّش، –ون	inspector
شاهِد عِيان، شُهود عِيان	eyewitness

رَئيس، رُؤَساء	president
وَزير، وُزَراء	minister
رَئيس الوُزَراء	prime minister (PM)
مَنْصِب رِئاسة الوُزَراء	the office of prime minister
نائِب، نُوّاب	member of parliament (MP), delegate
سِياسِيّ، ־ون	politician
قائِد، قُوّاد \ قادة	leader
زَعيم، زُعَماء	"
مَرْجِع، مَراجِع	authority (e.g. cleric)
مُسْتَشار، ־ون	consultant
مُحَلِّل، ־ون	analyst
خَبير، خُبَراء	expert
مُتَخَصِّص، ־ون	specialist, expert
مُراقِب، ־ون	observer; censor
ناقِد، ־ون \ نُقّاد	critic
نَظير، نُظَراء	counterpart, peer
ثائِر، ثُوّار	rebel, insurgent, revolutionary
مُتَمَرِّد، ־ون	"
مُنْشَقّ، ־ون	dissident

إرْهابيّ، ‑ون	terrorist
عَدُوّ، أَعْداء	enemy
عَدُوّ قَوْميّ رقْم ١	public enemy number one
مُنافِس، ‑ون	rival, competitor
خَصْم، خُصُوم	adversary
مُؤَيِّد، ‑ون	supporter
مُتَعاطِف، ‑ون	sympathiser
ناشِط \ مُنَشِّط، ‑ون	activist
مُسْتَوْطِن، ‑ون	settler
مُساعِد، ‑ون	aide, associate
مُتَشائِم، ‑ون	pessimist
مُتَفائِل، ‑ون	optimist
عُضْو، أَعْضاء	member
عُضْويّة	membership
رَهينة، رَهائِن	hostage
مَلِك، مُلُوك	king
مَلِكة، ‑ات	queen
عاهِل، عَواهِل	monarch
وَلِي العَهْد	Crown Prince

صاحِب الجَلالة	His Majesty
سُلْطان، سَلاطين	sultan
أَمير، أُمَراء	prince
والٍ، وُلاة	governor, ruler
خادِم الحَرَمَين الشَرِيفَين	Guardian of the Two Holy Shrines (i.e. Saudi king)
سَفير، سُفَراء	ambassador
أَمين عامّ	secretary general
مُتَحَدِّث باسْم	spokesperson
ناطِق باسْم	"
رائِد، رُوّاد	pioneer
جُمْهوريّة، ـات	republic
دَوْلة، دُوَل	state
وَطَن، أَوْطان	nation, homeland
شَعْب، شُعوب	a people
قَوْم، أَقْوام	"
بِلاد، بُلْدان	country
دُوَل نامية	developing countries
دُوَل مُتَخَلِّفة	developing (lit. backward) countries

دُوَل مُتَقَدِّمة	developed countries
دَوْلة قَوْميّة	nation-state
عاصِمة، عَواصِم	capital (geographical)
الدُوَل العُظْمَى	the Superpowers
دُوَل الخليج	the Gulf States
الأراضي المُحْتَلّة	the Occupied Territories
الضفّة الغَرْبيّة	the West Bank
قطاع غَزّة	the Gaza Strip
الاحْتلال	the Occupation
مُخَيَّم، –ات	(refugee) camp
مُسْتَوْطَنات	settlements
حُقوق الإنْسان	human rights
دَوائِر سياسيّة	political circles
أوْساط سياسيّة	"
مَصالِح مُرَسَّخة	entrenched interests
حَياة عامّة	public life
دُسْتور، دَساتير	constitution
وَثيقة، وَثائِق	draft bill, charter; document
مَرْسوم، مَراسيم	act, decree

سِياسة، –ات	policy
مَبْدأ، مَبادِئ	principle
تَيّار، –ات	trend, current
اِتِّجاه، –ات	"
اِخْتِلاف، –ات	difference
فَرْق، فُروق	"
فارِق، فَوارِق	difference, distinction
تَشابُه، –ات	similarity
بَرْنامَج، بَرامِج	programme
إصْلاح، –ات	reform
تَحْديث	modernisation
حَقيبة، حَقائِب	(ministerial) portfolio
تَوَلَّى حَقيبة	to take over the portfolio of (+ idafah)
تَعْديل وِزاريّ	cabinet reshuffle
أَوْراق اِعْتِماد	credentials
سَلام	peace
مُصالحة	conciliation
عَفْو عَن	amnesty for
حَلّ، حُلول	solution

حَلّ وَسَط	compromise
تَسْوية مَطالب	settlement of demands
تَسْوية سِلْميّة	peace settlement
مُعاهَدة سلام	peace treaty/peace accord
عَمَليّة سلام	peace process
تَعَهُّد، –ات بِ	pledge
اتِّفاق \ اتِّفاقيّة، –ات	agreement
حِلْف	pact, alliance
تَقارُب	rapprochement
عُزْلة \ عَزْل	isolation
ائْتِلاف	coalition
تَنْسيق بَين	alignment
حِوار، –ات	dialogue
شِعار، –ات	slogan, watchword
قِمّة، قِمَم	summit
مُؤْتَمَر، –ات	conference, congress
اجْتِماع، –ات	meeting, gathering
لِقاء، –ات	meeting
مُواجَهة، –ات	encounter

مُفاوَضات	negotiations
مُباحَثات \ مُحادَثات	talks, discussions
مُشاوَرة، –ات	consultation
مُناقَشة، –ات	discussion
مُبادَرة، –ات	initiative
خِيار، –ات	choice, option
اقْتِراح، –ات \ مُقْتَرَحات	suggestion
نَصيحة، نَصائِح	advice
رَدّ فِعْل، رُدود فِعْل \ أَفْعال	reaction
إجْراءات	measures
إجْراءات اسْتِثْنائِيّة	exceptional measures
مُسْتَجِدّات	innovations, recent measures
بذل يبذُل بَذْل جَهْداً \ جُهوداً	to exert effort
جَوْلة، –ات	round (of talks); tour
دَوْرة، –ات	round (of talks)
دَوْرة بَرْلَمانِيّة	parliamentary term/session
جَلْسة، –ات	session, sitting
مَرْحَلة، مَراحِل	stage, phase

تَقْدير لِ	appreciation of/for
عَلاقات ثُنائيّة	bilateral relations
عَلاقات ثُلاثيّة	trilateral relations
عَلاقات مُتَعَدِّدة الأَطْراف	multi-lateral relations
تَطْبيع العَلاقات	the normalisation of relations
أعاد\ قطع العَلاقات الدِبْلوماسيّة مَع	to resume/cut diplomatic relations with
ضَغْط، ضُغوط	pressure
تَوَتُّر، –ات	tension
تَرَدُّد	hesitation
تَقَدُّم	progress
تَخَلُّف	backwardness
الحالة الراهنة	the status quo
تَدَهْوُر	decline, slump, breakdown
اسْتِقْلال	independence
وَحْدة	unity
ثَوْرة، –ات	revolution
انْقِلاب، –ات	revolt, coup
حالة الطَوارِئ	state of emergency

مُحاوَلة اغْتِيال	assassination attempt
ادِّعاء، –ات	allegation
مُهاتَرة	abuse, insult, bickering
اسْتِنْكار	disapproval, horror
صِمام الأمان	safety valve
مُنافَسات طائِفيّة	sectarian rivalries
اسْتِقالة	withdrawal, dissolution; retirement, resignation
واجَه	to encounter, face
ثار يَثور ثَوْرة	to revolt
تَظاهَر	to demonstrate
قاوَم	to resist
عارَض	to oppose
رفض يرفُض رَفْض	to reject, refute, refuse
صارَع	to fight, struggle
ناضَل	"
كافَح	"
نازَع	"
قاتَل	"
منع يمنَع مَنْع ه من \ عن	to prevent s.t./s.o. from

بذر يبذُر بُذورَ الفِتْنة والشقاق	to sow the seeds of conflict
نافَس عَلَى	to contend, compete for
انْهار يَنْهار انْهيار	to fall, collapse
أَسْقَط النظام	to topple the regime
سَلَّم السُلْطة	to hand over power/authority
نقل ينقُل نَقْل السُلْطة إلَى	to transfer power to
أَعاد الديموقراطيّة	to reinstate democracy
تَوَلَّى	to take over, control
اِسْتَوْلَى عَلَى	to overwhelm, overcome
طغَى يَطْغَى طَغْي \ طُغْيان عَلَى	to seize, overcome, terrorise
سَيْطَر عَلَى	to dominate, control, seize
قمع يقمَع قَمْع	to suppress, repress
تَحَرَّش بِ	to harass
عَلَّق	to suspend
أزال يُزيل إزالة	to remove, sideline, get rid of
هَمَّش	to marginalise
أَلْغَى يُلْغي إلْغاء	to abolish

أَقال يُقيل إقالة	to dismiss
عزل يعزل عَزْل	"
حلّ يحُلّ حَلّ نَفْسَه	to dissolve itself
فَكَّك	to disband s.t.
اِعْتَزَل من	to withdraw from
اِنْشَقّ عَن	to break away, secede, split off from
تَفَكَّك	to disintegrate, break up
وضع يَضعِ وَضْع حَدّاً لِ	to put an end to
أَنْهَى	to end s.t.
اِنْتَهَى	to end (intransitive)
أَفْسَح المَجال	to clear the way
اِغْتال يَغْتال اِغْتِيال	to assassinate
اِخْتَطَف	to take hostage, abduct
اِنْتَمى إلَى	to belong to
أَوْشَك عَلَى	to be on the point of
عقد يعقد عَقْد	to convene, hold (meeting)
اِنْعَقَد	to be convened
أَجْرَى يُجْري إجْراء	to hold (talks)
نَسَّق	to arrange

اِسْتَأْنَف	to resume
جَدَّد	to renew
حضر يحضُر حُضور	to attend, be present
اِسْتَغْرَق	to last
اِسْتَمَرّ	to continue
أَجَّل يُؤَجِّل تَأْجيل	to delay, postpone
أَخَّر يُؤَخِّر تَأْخير	"
تَأَخَّر	to be delayed
اِسْتَقْبَل	to receive (visitor)
اِلْتَقَى بِ	to meet with
قام يقوم قيام بِرِحْلة	to take/make a trip
قام بِزيارة رَسْمِيّة	to pay a state/official visit
بِدَعْوة مِن	at the invitation of
سافَر	to travel
وصل يَصِل وُصول إلَى	to arrive in
بلغ يبلُغ بُلوغ	to reach
غادَر	to depart
عاد يعود عَوْدة	to return
رجع يرجِع رُجوع	"

تَوَجَّهَ إِلَى	to head for
في طَريق عَوْدتِه مِن	on his way back from
في خِتام زيارتِه إِلَى	at the end of his visit to
اِخْتَتَم زيارةً	to conclude a visit
رافَق	to accompany
اِصْطَحَب	"
أَرْسَل	to send
بعث يبعَث بَعْث	"
قَدَّم	to present, offer
سَلَّم	to hand over
منح يمنَح مَنْح	to award, grant, confer
تَسَلَّم	to obtain, receive
حصل يحصُل حُصول عَلَى	to get hold of, obtain
تَلَقَّى	to receive, obtain, take
اتَّفَق عَلَى	to agree on
أَجْمَع عَلَى	"
وَقَّع	to sign
قَرَّر	to decide, resolve
عزم يعزِم عَزْم عَلَى	to decide on, determine

حَسَم يحسِم حَسْم	to settle, decide
سَوَّى يُسَوِّي تَسْوية	to settle
أَبْقَى خياراتِهِ مَفْتوحة	to keep one's options open
أَسْقَط خياراً	to rule out an option
شَكَّل يُشَكِّل تَشْكيل	to form, shape
أَقام	to set up, erect, hold
أَسَّس يُؤَسِّس تَأْسيس	to found, establish
ثَبَّت	to stabilise, secure
رَسَّخ	to entrench
عَزَّز	to strengthen
دعم يدعَم دَعْم	to support
سانَد	"
أَيَّد يُؤَيِّد تَأْييد	to support s.o.
شَجَّع ه عَلَى	to encourage s.o. to do s.t.
مال يميل مَيْل إلَى	to lean towards, favour
دعا يَدْعو دَعْوة ه إلَى	to call on s.o. to
طَوَّر	to develop s.t.
تَطَوَّر	to develop (intransitive)
نَـمَّى	to promote, develop s.t.

تَنَمَّى	to grow, develop (intransitive)
وَسَّع	to expand s.t.
تَوَسَّع	to expand (intransitive)
حَوَّل \ غَيَّر	to change, transform s.t.
تحَوَّل \ تَغَيَّر	to change (intransitive)
حَسَّن	to improve s.t.
تَحَسَّن	to improve (intransitive)
قام يَقوم قيام بِ	to undertake
أَدار يُدير إدارة	to direct, administer
اتَّخَذ	to adopt (e.g. measures)
اعْتَنَق	to embrace (doctrine; person)
وَجَّه ه إلَى	to orientate s.t. towards
أَشْرَف عَلَى	to supervise, oversee, watch over
راقَب	to observe, watch, censor
مَحَّص	to scrutinise
دَقَّق	"
أَصْبَح أَمْراً واقِعاً	to become a reality
طرأ يطرأ طَرْء \ طُروء عَلَى	to befall, happen to s.o.

جَرى يجري جَرْي	to occur, happen
حدث يحدُث حَدَث	"
وقع يَقَع وُقوع	"
بدا يَبْدو	to seem
ظهر يظهَر ظُهور	to emerge, appear, seem
عاد إلَى الظُهور	to reappear, re-emerge
حَقَّق	to fulfil, realise
نَفَّذ	to implement, carry out
اِرْتَكَب	to commit, perpetrate
مارَس	to practise
مَزيد مِن	more of
بِرِئاسة	under the leadership of (+ idafah)
بِقيادة	"
بِزَعامة	"
سِيادة	sovereignty
اتَّخَذ خَطَوات	to take steps
دَفْعة قَويّة في	a strong step in
الاِتِّجاه الصَحيح	the right direction
طَفْرة نَوْعيّة	quantum leap

نُقْطة تحَوُّل	turning point
كان مَضْرِبَ المَثَل	to be exemplary/a byword
فرض يفرُض فَرْض عُقوبات	to impose sanctions
رفع يرفَع رَفْع عُقوبات	to lift sanctions
طلب يطلُب طلَب اللُجوءَ السياسيّ	to seek political asylum
حرْمان مِن	prevention of
ربط يربُطِ رَبْط بَين	to link, unite
ارْتَبَط بِ	to be linked to
تَعَلَّق بِ	to be related to
راوَح بَين	to fluctuate between
ضغط يضغَط ضَغْط عَلَى	to put pressure on
خَفَّف مِن	to moderate, diminish, ease
تَضاءَل	to fade, dwindle, diminish
خطف يخطَف خَطْف الأضْواء	to snatch the limelight
عانَى مِن	to suffer from
أُصِيب يُصاب إصابة بِ	to be afflicted by (Arabic passive)

3. ELECTIONS

انْتِخاب، –ات	election
انْتِخابات فَرْعِيّة	by-elections
انْتِخابات عامّة	general elections
انْتِخابات رئاسيّة	presidential elections
انْتِخابات مُبكِّرة	early elections
اسْتِطْلاع رَأْي	opinion poll
اقْتِراع، –ات	ballot
اقْتِراع ثقة	vote of confidence
حَمْلة، حَمَلات	campaign
مُرَشَّح، –ون	candidate
مُرَشَّح مُسْتقِلّ	independent candidate
شَخْصيّة، –ات	personality
صورة، صُوَر	image
شُهْرة	reputation
اشْتِهار	notoriety
شَعْبيّة	popularity
تَراجُع في الشعْبيّة	a decline in popularity
أحْزاب مُتَصارِعة	contending parties

وَلاء لِ	loyalty to
غَيْر الناخِبِين	non-voters
مُسَجَّلُون في قَوائِمِ الاقْتِراع	registered voters
الناخِبون	the electorate
مَقْعَد، مَقاعِد	seat
صَوْت أَصْوات	vote
انْتِصار، –ات	victory
تَزْوير الانْتِخابات	election-rigging
انْتِخابات حُرَّة ونَظيفة	free and fair elections
الحِزْب الأَكْثَر اتِّساعاً	the most widespread party
الحِزْب الأَسْرَع نمُوّاً	the fastest-growing party
دِعاية	propaganda
أَجْرَى انْتِخابات	to hold elections
أَجَّل انْتِخابات	to delay elections
أَلْغَى انْتِخابات	to cancel elections
صَوَّت	to vote
أَحْجَم عَن	to abstain from
فاز يفوز فَوْز في	to gain, win votes
أَحْرَز انْتِصاراً ساحِقاً	to win a landslide victory

أَحْرَزَ أَغْلَبِيّةً ساحِقةً	to secure an overwhelming majority
أخذ يأْخُذ أَخْذ أَعِنّةَ الحُكومة	to take up the reins of government
وصل يَصِل وُصول إلى السُّلْطة	to come to power
رَشَّح	to appoint
نَصَّب	"

4. MILITARY

المُؤَسَّسة الْعَسْكَرِيّة	the military
العَسْكَرِيّون	"
جَيْش، جيُوش	army
القُوّات المُسلَّحة	the armed forces
القُوّات	the troops
رُكْن، أَرْكان	military staff
جُنْدِيّ، جنُود	soldier
مَدَنِيّ، –ون	civilian
المُشاة	the infantry (Arabic pl.)
بَحّار، –ون \ بَحّارة	sailor
جُنْدِيّ مُشاة البَحْرِيّة	marine
طَيّار، –ون	airman, pilot
مِظَلّيّ، –ون	paratrooper
قانص، قُنّاص	sniper
بَطَل، أَبْطال	hero
حَليف، حُلَفاء	ally, confederate
لِواء، أَلْوِية	general (rank); flag
رَئِيس الأرْكان	chief of staff

رُتْبة، رُتَب	rank, grade
قُوّة جَوِّيّة	air force
قُوّات بَرِّيّة	ground forces
قُوّات احْتِياطِيّة	reserves
قُوّة خاصّة	commando, special troop
قُوّة خَفيفة	light/mobile task force
قِطَعات قتاليّة	combat troops
قُوّات حِفْظ السَلام	peacekeeping forces
قُوّات التَحالُف	the Allied Forces
قُوّة دفاعيّة	defence force
قُوّة هُجُوميّة ضاربة	strike force
قُوّة رَدْع	deterrent force
فَصيلة، فَصائِل	cell, squad
فَصيلة الإعْدام	execution squad, firing squad
دَوْرِيّة، –ات	patrol
وَحْدة، وَحَدات	(military) unit
سِرْب، أَسْراب	squadron
كَتيبة، كَتائِب	battalion
سِلاح، أَسْلِحة	weapon

أَسْلِحة خَفيفة \ صَغيرة	small arms
ذَخيرة	ammunition
مِظلّة، –ات	parachute
تَرْسانة، –ات	arsenal
أَسْلِحة نَوَوِيّة	nuclear weapons
أَسْلِحة ذَكِيّة	precision weapons
أَسْلِحة الدَمارِ الشامِل	weapons of mass destruction (WMD)
صاروخ، صَواريخ	missile, rocket
صاروخ مُضادّ للطائِرات	anti-aircraft missile
صاروخ تَمْويهيّ	decoy missile
صاروخ طَوّاف	cruise missile
صاروخ سَطْح – جَوّ	surface-to-air missile
صاروخ بَعيد \ قَصير المَدَى	long-/short-range missile
قَذيفة عابِرة للقارّات	intercontinental ballistic missile
قاذفة الصَواريخ	rocket/missile launcher
نَسيفة، نَسائِف	torpedo
قُنْبُلة، قَنابِل	bomb
أداة تَفْجير	explosive device

مُتَفَجِّرات	explosives
قُنْبُلة يَدَويّة	hand grenade
قُنْبُلة نَوَويّة	nuclear bomb
قُنْبُلة ذَرّيّة	atomic bomb
قُنْبُلة عُنْقوديّة	cluster bomb
قُنْبُلة حارقة	incendiary bomb
قَذيفة هاوُن، قَذائِف هاوُن	mortar bomb
لَغَم \ لُغْم، أَلْغام	mine
رَصاصة، –ات \ رَصاص	bullet
مِدْفَع، مَدافِع	gun
مُسَدَّس، –ات	revolver
مِدْفَع رَشّاش	machine gun
رَشّاش قَصير	sub-machine gun
بُنْدُقيّة آليّة	automatic rifle
سِلاح قَذّافيّ	ballistic weapon
قطْعة مِدْفَعيّة	(piece of) artillery
قَصْف مِدْفَعيّ	artillery fire
قَصْف صاروخيّ	rocket fire
شَظايا	shrapnel (Arabic pl.)

إشْعاع	radiation
انْفِجار \ تَفْجير \ تَفَجُّر	explosion
عَصْف	blast
قَصْف	bombardment, shelling
قَصْف دَقيق \ ذَكيّ	precision bombing
ضَرْبة وِقائيّة	preemptive strike
اسْتِخْدام القُوّة	use of force
غِطاء جَوّيّ	air cover
مِنْطَقة حَظْر جَوّيّ	no-fly zone
ناقِلة جُنود مُدَرَّعة	armoured personnel carrier
دَبّابة، ـات	tank
جَرّافة، ـات	bulldozer
طائِرة عَمُوديّة	helicopter
طائِرة مِرْوَحيّة	"
هليكوبتر	"
غَوّاصة مُضادّة للطائِرات	anti-aircraft submarine
حامِلة طائِرات	aircraft carrier
طائِرة مُقاتِلة	fighter aircraft
مُدَمِّرة، ـات	destroyer

سَفينة حَرْبيّة، سُفُن حَرْبيّة	warship, frigate
بارجة، بَوارِج	"
زَوْرَق حَرْبيّ، زَوارِق حَرْبيّة	gunboat
نَسّافة، –ات	torpedo boat
أُسْطول، أَساطيل	fleet
قَاعدة عَسْكَريّة، قَواعد عَسْكَريّة	military base
مَقَرّ، مَقارّ	headquarters (HQ)
مَوْقِع اسْتراتيجيّ، مَواقِع اسْتراتيجيّة	strategic point
مِنْطَقة القتال، مَناطق القتال	combat zone
مِنْطَقة خالية مِن الأسْلِحة النَوَويّة	nuclear-free zone
انْتِشار الأسْلِحة النَوَويّة	nuclear proliferation
جِهاز طَرْد مَرْكَزيّ	centrifugal system
تَخْصيب اليورانيوم	enrichment of uranium
حَرْب، حُروب	war (Arabic fem.)
حَرْب أَهْليّة	civil war
حَرْب عِصابات	guerilla warfare

فِي حالةِ الحَرْب	at war
مَسْرَح الحَرْب	theatre of war
مَيدان العَمَلِيّات	field of operations
مُناوَرة، –ات	manoeuvre
اسْتِطْلاع	reconnaissance
اسْتِعْراض \ عَرْض	parade
مَعْرَكة، مَعارِك	battle
خَطَر، أَخْطار \ مَخاطِر	danger
أَمْن	safety
وَقْف إِطْلاقِ النار	ceasefire
تَجْريد مِنَ السِلاح	disarmament; demilitarisation
أَعْمال العُنْف	acts of violence
أَعْمال التَخْريب	acts of sabotage
عَمَلِيّة انْتحارِيّة	suicide bombing
سَيّارة مُفَخَّخة	car bomb (lit. booby-trapped car)
مَجْزَرة، مَجازِر	massacre
إبادة جَماعِيّة	genocide
مَصْرَع، مَصارِع	death; battleground
مَقْتَل	murder, killing

قَطْع الرَأْس	beheading
تَدَخُّل عَسْكَريّ	military intervention
إصابة، –ات	injury
جُرْح، جُروح \ جِراح	"
جِنازة، –ات \ جَنائِز	funeral (procession)
ضَحِيّة، ضَحايا	victim
جَريح، جَرْحَى	wounded, injured (person)
قَتيل، قَتْلَى	dead (person)
أَسير، أَسْرَى	captured (person), prisoner
مُحْتَجَز، –ون	detainee
مُنَفِّذ عَمَلِيّة اِنْتِحارِيّة	suicide bomber
مُباغَتة، –ات	surprise attack, raid
هُجوم بَرّيّ	ground offensive, land attack
هُجوم بَرْمائِيّ	amphibious attack
هُجوم إرْهابيّ	terrorist attack
هُجوم مُسَلَّح عَلَى	armed attack on
هُجوم مُضادّ	counter attack
كَمين	ambush
تَكْتيكات	tactics

اعْتِداءات عَلَى	aggressions against
رَدَّ انْتِقامِيّ عَلَى	revenge for
عَلَى مَتْن	on board (a ship/aircraft)
	(+ idafah)
في وَضْع اسْتِعْداد لِ	in a state of readiness for
مُنْتَشِر	deployed (lit. spreading out)
عُدْوانِيّ \ عَدائِيّ	hostile
انْعِكاسات \ عَواقِب	repercussions
حَشَدَ يَحْشُدُ حَشْد	to mobilise, call up,
	to accumulate
عَبَّأَ	to mobilise
قام بتَعْبِئة	" (+ idafah)
حَشَّدَ	to amass (especially troops)
جَنَّدَ	to draft, conscript, mobilise
اسْتَدْعَى	to call up
عَزَّزَ القُوّات	to reinforce the troops
نَشَرَ يَنْشُرُ نَشْر	to deploy
تَفَقَّدَ	to inspect
فَجَّرَ	to explode s.t.
تَفَجَّرَ	to explode (intransitive)

دَمَّر	to destroy
هدم يهدم هَدْم	"
أَباد	to annihilate
أَفْنَى	"
تَبادَل إطْلاقَ النار	to exchange fire
أوْدَى بِحَياة	to claim the life/lives of (+ idafah)
اُسْتُشْهِد	to be martyred (Arabic passive)
أُصيبَ بِجُروح خَطيرة \ طَفيفة	to suffer serious/minor injuries (Arabic passive)
هجم يهجُم هُجوم عَلَى	to attack
غزا يَغْزو غَزْو	to attack, invade, raid
شنّ يشُنّ شَنّ هُجوماً \ حَمْلةً	to launch an attack/ a campaign
أطْلَق	to launch (missile, torpedo, etc.)
اقْتَحَم	to storm
تَسَلَّل إلَى	to infiltrate
تَوَغَّل في	to advance further, to penetrate deeply into

حاصَر	to besiege, surround
فتح يفتَح فَتْح النار	to open fire
أَطْلَق النار	"
دافَع عَن	to defend
حمَى يحمي حِماية ه مِن	to protect s.t. against
اِنْسَحَب	to withdraw (intransitive)
جلا يجلو جَلاء عَن	to evacuate, pull out of
أَجْلَى	to evacuate (transitive)
اِسْتَسْلَم	to surrender
اِحْتَجَز	to detain
أَفْرَج عَن	to release
أَطْلَق	"
أَطْلَق سَراحَهُ	to set s.o. free
أَخْلَى سَبِيلَهُ	to let s.o. go
اِسْتَأْنَف القِتال	to resume fighting
قاوَم	to resist
خَطَّط	to plan
تَآمَر	to plot
اِسْتَهْدَف تَحْديداً	to target specifically

نصب ينصُب نَصْب حَواجِز عَلَى الطُرُق	to erect road blocks
فرض يفرُض فَرْض حِصاراً عَلَى	to impose a cordon/ blockade on
انْدَلَع	to break out (war)
بوسْعِهِ أَن	to be in s.o.'s power to
احْتَلَّ	to occupy
أَحَلَّ مَحَلَّهُ	to take the place of
اخْتَرَقَ الحُدود	to cross the border(s)
قَدَّر حَجْمَ القُوّات بِ	to estimate the strength of forces at
اسْتَخْلَص المعْلومات	to debrief

5. ECONOMICS

صُنْدوق النَقْدِ الدَولِيّ	IMF (International Monetary Fund)
البَنْك الدَولِيّ	the World Bank
البَنْك المَرْكَزِيّ الأُورُبِّيّ	the European Central Bank
الاحْتِياطِيّ الاِتِّحادِيّ	the Federal Reserve
السوق المُشْتَرَكة	the Common Market
سوق سَوْداء	black market
سوق حُرّة	free market
سوق النَقْد	the Stock Exchange
البورصة	"
أسْواق الصَرْف	exchange markets
أسْواق العُمْلات الأَجْنَبِيّة	foreign currency markets
احْتِياطات النَقْد الأَجْنَبِيّ	foreign currency reserves
قِطاع عامّ	public sector
قِطاع خاصّ	private sector
تَكامُل اقْتِصادِيّ	economic integration
حَجْم التِجارة	volume of trade
تَبادُل تِجارِيّ	trade exchange

حَظْر تِجاريّ	trade embargo
عُقوبات اقْتِصاديّة	economic sanctions
لَدَى إغْلاق التَداوُل	at the close of trade
عُمْلة صَعْبة	hard currency
عُمْلة سَهْلة	soft currency
رَأْس مال، رُؤوس أمْوال	capital
رَأْسْمال، رَساميل	"
دَخْل	income
قُوّة الشِراء	purchasing power
احْتِكار، –ات	monopoly; cartel
قُوّات السُوق	market forces
تَنافُس	competition
قُدْرة تَنافُسيّة	competitiveness
سِعْر الصَرْف	exchange rate
سِعْر الفائِدة	interest rate
فائِدة مُيَسَّرة	preferential rate of interest
سِعْر البَيع	retail price
سِعْر اليورو مُقابِلَ الدولار	the price of the euro against the dollar
سَهْم، أَسْهُم	share

سَنَد، –ات	bond
مُشْتَقّات	derivatives
ضَريبة، ضَرائب	tax
ضَريبة الدَخْل	income tax
ضَريبة الاسْتِهْلاك	value added tax (VAT)
ضَريبة القيمة المُضافة	"
ضَريبة الأرْباح الرَأْسْماليّة	capital gains tax
ضَريبة التَّرِكات	inheritance tax
بالمائة \ بالمئة	per cent
اسْتِثْمار، –ات	investment
وَديعة، وَدائع	deposit
أَصْل، أُصول	asset
عائِد، –ات	dividend, return
إيراد، –ات	revenue, profit
حَصيلة، حَصائل	income, yield
مَبْلَغ، مَبالغ	amount
رِبْح، أرْباح	profit
مُرْبِح	profitable
مُفْلِس، مَفاليس	bankrupt

تَكاليف	costs
نَفَقات	expenses
إجْماليّ	total, gross
صافي	net
بَعْد اسْتِبْعاد أَثَرِ التَضَخُّم	in real terms
مُساندة الأسْعار من طَرْفِ الدَوْلة	price control
اسْتِقْرار الأسْعار	price stability
القَرْية الكَوْنيّة	the global village
عَوْلَة	globalisation
دَوْلة الرَفاه	the welfare state
غَسيل الأمْوال	money laundering
رُكود	recession
تَدَهْوُر	decline, slump
تَضَخُّم	inflation
مُعَدَّل التَضَخُّم	rate of inflation
تَخْفيض القيمة	devaluation
تَكَهُّن، -ات	forecasting
مُضارَبة	speculation

عَدَم الاسْتِقْرار	instability
تَذَبْذُب	fluctuation
إفْلاس	bankruptcy
مُسْتَوَى المَعيشة	standard of living
دَيْن، دُيُون	debt
مَدْيُونيّة	debt/indebtedness
دَيْن مُسْتَحَقّ	outstanding debt
قَرْض، قُرُوض	loan
فَتْرة سَماح	grace period
عَجْز في ميزانيّة الدَوْلة	budget deficit
عَجْز تِجاريّ	trade deficit
قيمة العَجْز	the amount of the deficit
فائِض، فَوائِض	surplus
سُيولة	liquidity
اقْتِصاد الحَجْم	economy of scale
العَام الماليّ \ السَّنة الماليّة	the financial year
رَقْم قِياسيّ	record figure
إحْصائيّات	statistics
مُؤَشِّر، –ات	index, indicator

سِلْعة، سِلَع	commodity
سِلَع اسْتِهْلاكيّة	consumer goods
مُعَدَّل اِسْتِهْلاك	the average consumption of (+ idafah)
وَزير الماليّة	finance minister
مُـمَوِّل، –ون	financier
اقتِصاديّ، –ون	economist
مُعامِل، –ون	trader, dealer
سِمْسار، سَماسِرة	broker
مُضارِب، –ون	speculator
مُساهِم، –ون	shareholder
مُسْتَثْمِر، –ون	investor
مُسْتَهْلِك، –ون	consumer
شَريك تِجاريّ، شُرَكاء تِجاريّون	trade partner
نَفَّذ عُقوبات اِقْتِصاديّة	to apply economic sanctions
مَوَّل	to finance
شَغَّل رَأْسْمالاً	to invest capital
أَنْفَق	to spend
أَضاع	to squander

كَلَّف	to cost
كَثَّف	to consolidate
أمَّن	to insure
ازْدَهَر	to blossom, flourish
رفع يرفَع رفْع \ خَفَّض الضَرائِب	to raise/lower taxes
خَفَّف العَجْز في الميزانيّة	to reduce the budget deficit
دخل يدخُل دُخول حَيِّزَ التَنْفيذ	to come into effect
نَشَّط الاقْتِصاد	to stimulate the economy
سدّ يسُدّ سَدّ \ سَداد دَيْناً	to repay a debt
اسْتَحَقّ	to become payable
أفْلَس	to become bankrupt
ربط يربِط رَبْط العُمْلة بِالدولار	to tie the currency to the dollar

6. TRADE & INDUSTRY

أُوبك	OPEC
مُنَظَّمة الدُوَل المُصَدِّرة للنَفْط	Organisation of the Petroleum Exporting Countries
الدُوَل المُنْتِجة للنَفْط غَيْر الأعْضاء في أُوبك	non-OPEC
مُنَظَّمة التِجارة العالميّة	WTO (World Trade Organisation)
مَجْموعة الثَماني	G8 (Group of 8)
تِجارة	trade
صِناعة	industry
صادِرات	exports
وارِدات	imports
مَجْموعة، –ات	conglomerate
مُساهَمة، –ات	corporation
شِراكة، –ات	partnership
انْدِماج، –ات	merger
هَيْكَل، هَياكِل	structure
مَصْنَع، مَصانِع	factory

مِصْفاة، مَصاف	refinery
بِئْر نَفْطيّة، آبار نَفْطيّة	oil well (Arabic fem.)
نَفْط خام	crude oil
مَعْروض نَفْطيّ	oil supply
إنْتاج النَفْط	oil production
بِرْميل، بَراميل	barrel
وَقُود	fuel (petrol/gas for cars)
مَوادّ خام \ خامات	raw materials
مَوادّ غذائيّة	foodstuffs
مَوارِد طَبيعيّة	natural resources
مَعْدَن، مَعادِن	mineral
مَنْجَم، مَناجِم	mine
اليَد العامِلة	the workforce
القُوَى العامِلة	"
مُوَظَّف، -ون	employee, functionary
عامِل، عُمّال	worker
عاطِل، -ون	unemployed person
مُدير، -ون \ مُدَراء	director, head
مُدير عامّ	director general

رَجُل أَعْمال، رِجال أَعْمال	businessman
وَظيفة، وَظائِف	job
زِيادة الأُجور	wage increase
بَطالة	unemployment
إضْراب	strike
نِقابة، –ات	trade union
اتِّحاد نِقابيّ	"
بُنْية تَحْتيّة	infrastructure
سِعْر التَشْغيل	running cost
دَعْم حُكوميّ	government subsidy
تَعاقُد، –ات	contract
صَفْقة، صَفَقات	deal
خَسارة، خَسائِر	loss
ضَرَر، أَضْرار	damage
تَأْمين، –ات	insurance
قَيْد، قُيود	restriction
مُرونة	flexibility
مَحَطّة تَوْليدِ الكَهْرَباء	power station
طاقة	energy

تَلَوُّث	pollution
أَمْطار سَوْداء	black rain
حماية البيئة	environmental protection
حَمْلة التَسْويق	marketing campaign
مَوْقِع شبَكة الإنْتَرْنَت، مَواقِع شبَكة الإنْتَرْنَت	website
مَعْلوماتيّة	IT (information technology)
صدَّر	to export
اسْتَوْرَد \ ورَّد	to import
وزَّع	to distribute
زَوَّد	to supply
اسْتَقال	to retire, resign
وظَّف	to employ
شغَّل	"
أَقال	to dismiss (from job)
أَدار يُدير إدارة	to direct
زاد يزيد زيادة	to increase s.t.
ازْداد	to increase (intransitive)
زاد يزيد زيادة عَن	to exceed

عَوَّض عَن	to compensate for
خَصْخَص	to privatise
رفع يرفَع رَفْع القُيودَ الحكوميّة	to deregulate (lit. to lift government restrictions)
رَعَى يرعَى رَعْي	to sponsor
تَعامَل مَع	to do business with

7. LAW & ORDER

قانون، قَوانين	law
بَنْد، بُنود	article (of law)
مَحْكَمة، مَحاكِم	court
مَحْكَمة العَدْل الدَولِيّة	the International Court of Justice
مَحْكَمة عُلْيا	high court
الحَرَس الوَطَنيّ	the national guard
قُوّات الأمْن	the security forces
الشُرْطة العَسْكَريّة	the military police
المُخابَرات	the intelligence service
سُلْطة قَضائِيّة	judicial power
سُلْطة تَشْريعيّة	legislative power
إجْراءات أمْنيّة	security measures
تُهْمة، تُهَم	accusation
بِتُهَم	on charges of (+ idafah)
مَحْكوم عَلَيه بِ	sentenced to
مُدان بِ	convicted of
اسْتِجابةً لِ	in response to

مُحْتَجّ، –ون	protester
مُتَظاهِر، –ون	demonstrator
مُهَرِّب، –ون	smuggler
سَجين سِياسيّ، سُجَناء سِياسيّون	political prisoner
مُجْرِم، –ون	criminal
مُشْتَبَه بِهِ، مُشْتَبَه بِهِم	suspect
مُسَلَّح، –ون	gunman
عِصابة، –ات	gang
شَبَكة، –ات	network
جَريمة، جَرائِم	crime, offence
جِناية، –ات	crime, felony
اِنْتِهاك، –ات	abuse, violation
قَسْوة	abuse, cruelty
جَريمة القَتْل	homicide
مَقْتَل بِالرَصاص	(fatal) shooting
سَرِقة / سِرْقة، –ات	burglary, theft
مُحاوَلة اِنْقِلابيّة	attempted coup
اِحْتِجاج، –ات	protest

تَهْديد، –ات	threat
تحَدٍّ، تحَدّيات	challenge
تَظاهُر \ مظاهرة، –ات	demonstration
اشْتِباك، –ات	clash, scuffle
مُخَدِّرات	drugs
مَسْروقات	stolen goods
تَحْقيق جِنائيّ، –ات جِنائيّة	criminal investigation
ذُو سَوابِق	s.o. with a (criminal) record
اِنْحِراف	delinquency
مَشْروعيّة	legality
تَرْخيص، تَراخيص	permit, licence
كامِل الأهْليّة	legally competent
عَديم الأهْليّة	legally incompetent
جِنائيّ	criminal (adj.)
عِقابيّ	punitive, penal
جَلْسة المَحْكَمة	court hearing
رَأْي يُعَدّ غَيْر مُلْزِم	non-binding opinion
أَدان يُدين إدانة ه بِ	to convict s.o. of s.t.
طعن يطعَن طَعْن في	to contest, appeal against

اتَّهَم ه بِ	to accuse s.o. of s.t.
اِعْتَرَف بِ	to confess, admit
وَجَّه اتِّهامات ضدّ	to press charges against
حكم يحكُم حُكْم عَلَيْهِ بِالإعْدام	to sentence s.o. to death
حكم عَلَيْهِ بِالسِجْنِ المُؤَبَّد	to sentence to life imprisonment
أَعْدَم	to execute
أوْقَف \ وَقَّف	to arrest
اِعْتَقَل	"
قبض يقبِض قَبْض على	"
أَلْقَى القَبْض عَلَى	"
أساء المُعامَلة	to mistreat
أَبْعَد	to deport, expatriate, expel, exile
نفَى ينفي نَفْي	"
طرد يطرُد طَرْد	"
عاش يَعيش عَيْش في المَنْفَى	to live in exile
اِرْتَكَب	to commit (a crime)

وضع يَضع وَضْع في | to put on red alert
حال تَأَهُّب قُصْوَى

فرض يفرُض فَرْض حظْرَ | to impose a curfew
التَجَوُّل

أَعْلَن مَسْؤوليّتَهُ عَن | to claim/declare one's
responsibility for

نَظَّم | to organise

دعا يَدْعو دَعْوة إلَى | to call a strike
إضْراب

احْتَجّ عَلَى | to protest against

تَلاءَم مَع | to comply with

تَوَرَّط في | to be involved in

هَدَّد ه ب | to threaten s.o. with s.t.

8. DISASTER & AID

أَزْمة، أَزَمات	crisis
كارِثة، كَوارِث	disaster, catastrophe
مَأْساة، مآسٍ	tragedy
طارِئة، طَوارِئ	emergency
مَعُونة	aid
إغاثة	"
مُساعَدات	" (Arabic pl.)
وِكالة إغاثة اللاجِئِين	UNRWA (United Nations
للأمَم المُتَّحِدة	Relief and Works Agency)
دَعْم	support
مِنْحة، مِنَح	grant
عَطاء، أَعْطِية	gift
سَخاء	generosity
مُساعَدات غذائيّة	food aid
مُساعَدات فَنّيّة	technical aid
مُساعَدات ماليّة	financial aid
إلْغاء الدُّيون	debt cancellation
مُتَطَوِّع، -ون	volunteer

عامل الإغاثة، عُمّال ،	aid worker
هَيْئة المَعُونة	aid/relief organisation
مُنَظَّمة طَوْعيّة	voluntary organisation
مُنَظَّمة خَيريّة	charity
زَلْزال، زَلازل	earthquake
هَزّة أَرْضيّة، –ات أَرْضيّة	earth tremor, seismic shock
بمقْياس ريخْتَر	on the Richter scale
فَيَضان، –ات	flood
إعْصار، –ات	hurricane
تسونامي	tsunami
انْهِيار طيني، –ات طينيّة	mudslide
حَريق، حَرائق	fire
مَجاعة	famine
جَفاف	drought
سُوْء التَغْذية	malnutrition
قافلة الأغْذية	food convoy
شاحِنة، –ات	lorry, truck
خَيْمة، –ات \ خِيام	tent
إعادة الإسْكان	resettlement